ISBN 978-1-332-81832-7
PIBN 10467587

English
Français
Deutsche
Italiano
Español
Português

www.forgottenbooks.com

Mythology Photography **Fiction**
Fishing Christianity **Art** Cooking
Essays Buddhism Freemasonry
Medicine **Biology** Music **Ancient**
Egypt Evolution Carpentry Physics
Dance Geology **Mathematics** Fitness
Shakespeare **Folklore** Yoga Marketing
Confidence Immortality Biographies
Poetry **Psychology** Witchcraft
Electronics Chemistry History **Law**
Accounting **Philosophy** Anthropology
Alchemy Drama Quantum Mechanics
Atheism Sexual Health **Ancient History**
Entrepreneurship Languages Sport
Paleontology Needlework Islam
Metaphysics Investment Archaeology
Parenting Statistics Criminology
Motivational

OTHER BOOKS
By MRS S T RORER

MRS RORER'S COOK BOOK

nearly 600 pages of the choicest recipes in every department of cookery; bound in washable oil-cloth covers, $1 75

CANNING AND PRESERVING

paper covers, 40 cents . cloth, 75 cents

HOT WEATHER DISHES

paper covers, 40 cents : cloth, 75 cents

HOME CANDY MAKING

paper covers, 40 cents ; cloth, 75 cents

TWENTY QUICK SOUPS

FIFTEEN NEW WAYS FOR OYSTERS

HOW TO USE A CHAFING DISH

COLONIAL RECIPES

SANDWICHES

DAINTIES

Each of the above six volumes is bound in a different colored linen cloth, beautifully stamped in colors, price 25 cents each

ARNOLD AND COMPANY Publishers
PHILADELPHIA

DAINTIES

DAINTIES

By MRS S T RORER

PHILADELPHIA

ARNOLD AND COMPANY

Copyright 1894 by Mrs S T Rorer

Printed by
George H Buchanan and Company
Philadelphia

CONTENTS

PINEAPPLE HULNAH

Pare and remove the eyes from one large or two small pineapples; grate, rejecting the core. Mix four even tablespoonfuls of cornstarch with half cup granulated sugar; now add this to the pineapple, turn the whole into a double boiler and stir constantly until boiling hot and thick; add a tablespoonful of butter, or two of cocoanut cream, and turn into a fancy pudding mold. Stand in a cold place to harden. When ready to serve, turn on a pretty plate, heap whipped cream around, garnish with candied violets, and serve.

EAST INDIA CHARLOTTE

Put one pint of milk into a double
boiler. Moisten four tablespoonfuls
of cornstarch in a little cold milk,
add this to the hot milk, cook until
thick and smooth; add half cup of
sugar and one cup of grated cocoanut; mix and turn into a shallow
pan to cool. Do not have the mixture over one inch thick. When
cold and hard, with a round cutter,
cut the whole into cakes. Lift each
carefully and put it on the individual
dish on which it is to be served.

Cover quarter box of gelatin with
quarter cup of cold milk and soak
ten minutes. Stand over hot water
until dissolved, add it to one pint

of thick cream, add three-quarters cup of powdered sugar and teaspoonful of vanilla sugar. Make the cream icy cold and whip it to a froth. Put this in a pastry bag, using a star tube; force it around the cakes, in fancy designs. Heap blocks of a clear, bright jelly in the center, and, when cold again, serve.

CREAM CHERRIES

Put a half pound of granulated sugar and a half cup of water over the fire to boil. Stir until the sugar is dissolved, then boil carefully until you can spin a thread from the tine of a fork. Turn on a greased platter and when cool (not cold), stir with a spoon until it granulates and is perfectly white. Scrape the mixture together and knead it for a moment, then put it into a little saucepan, stand this in another of boiling water and stir constantly until it melts. If, then, you find it too thick, add, drop by drop, sufficient water to make it the right consistency. Have ready your little paper cases, or a cut-glass dish upon which you are going to serve the cherries. Select red, white and black cherries and allow them to remain in bunches on the stem. Dip, one at a time, carefully into the cream, which must be kept hot. Hold for an instant, and then heap gracefully on the plate, or, if they are single cherries, you may place at once in the little paper cases.

All kinds of small fruit are exceedingly pretty dipped in this way.

CREAM STRAWBERRIES

Make and melt the cream as directed in the preceding recipe. Select medium-sized ripe berries. Pull the hulls close to the stem, dip the berries down into the cream and then replace the hull. Put them at once into paper cases and stand them away for use, or these may also be heaped on a cut-glass dish. Strawberries, having a soft outside cover, will only keep a few hours.

Carpels of oranges, white grapes —in fact, all kinds of grapes—may be served in this way.

STUFFED DATES

Select the rich, dark dates and those that are in good shape. Split on one side and carefully remove the stone. In the place of the stone put quarter of an English walnut. Wrap the date over until it looks perfect and arrange neatly on a pretty plate.

CHERRIES IN JELLY

Select one quart of ripe red cherries. Stone them carefully, saving all the liquor that is lost during stoning. Put three teaspoonfuls of granulated gelatin in a half pint of cold water; let it soak while you are stoning the cherries. Now add the cherry juice to the gelatin. Stir over boiling water until the gelatin is thoroughly dissolved, and at the same time put a cup of sugar over the cherries. As soon as the gelatin has thoroughly melted strain it carefully over the cherries, mix and turn into a fancy mold. Stand away for two or three hours until congealed enough to hold its shape. This must not be stiff but just hold together.

COMPOTE OP PINEAPPLE

Peel, and pick apart with a silver fork one good-sized, very ripe pine-apple. Cover three teaspoonfuls or granulated gelatin with a half cup or cold water and soak for five minutes. Cut two good-sized oranges into halves, carefully remove the seeds, and then, with a spoon, take out each little carpel. Mix with the pineapple. Turn over this, one cup of granulated sugar. Mix until the sugar is thoroughly dissolved, then heat the gelatin over hot water, add it to the pineapple and orange, and turn into small individual molds. Stand away in a cold place for at least two hours. Turn out and serve, with whipped cream. This cannot stand too long, or it will become liquid.

CREAM JELLY

Put two teaspoonfuls of granulated gelatin into one pint of cream; add half cup of granulated sugar and teaspoonful of vanilla; stand in a cold place for ten minutes. Then stir over hot water until the cream is sufficiently hot to dissolve the gelatin. Strain, and when cool, not thick, add four tablespoonfuls of sherry. Turn into small individual molds and stand away on the ice. Serve icy cold.

18

BAVAROISE

Cover two teaspoonfuls of granulated gelatin with four tablespoonfuls of cold water. Put one and a half cups of cream in a double boiler with a teaspoonful of vanilla sugar; bring it to scalding point and then stand it aside for twenty minutes until the cream is thoroughly flavored with the vanilla. Add the gelatin to this and stir until dissolved. Now, mix a half cup of sugar, gradually, with the yolks of four eggs. Beat until light, add to the cream, and stir it over the fire in a double boiler until it begins to thicken. Be exceedingly careful not to curdle. Now strain this into a basin and stand it in a pan of cracked ice. Stir constantly until the mixture begins to thicken, then stir in half pint of cream that has been whipped to a stiff froth. Turn into a fancy mold and stand away on the ice.

When ready to serve, dip the mold quickly into a pan of hot water. Have ready any small, fresh fruit — raspberries, strawberries or peaches. Turn pudding out in the center of a plate, heap the fruit around the base of the pudding, and serve; or a border mold may be used, and fruit placed in the center.

PISTACH CREAM

Cover two teaspoonfuls of granulated gelatin with half cup of milk
to soak for ten minutes. Whip one
pint of cream, turn it into a pan and
stand it in another of cracked ice.
Add half cup of powdered sugar,
four tablespoonfuls of Madeira and
a half teaspoonful of bitter almond.
Stand the gelatin over hot water
until dissolved. Strain it into the
cream and stir carefully until the
mixture begins to thicken. Then
turn into a fancy mold and stand
away on the ice for two or three
hours. Remove the hulls from two
ounces of pistachio nuts and chop
them very, very fine. Put them in

a sieve. When you are ready to serve the cream, dip the mold quickly in hot water, loosen it from the edge and turn it in the center of the serving dish. Garnish the base with preserved green walnuts and sprinkle the pistachio nuts thickly over the top.

RICE A L'IMPERATRICE

Wash a half cup of rice through several cold waters, rubbing it well in the hands. Let it soak over night. Next morning when you are ready to make the dessert throw this rice into about one pint of boiling water. Stand it on the back part of the stove where it cannot possibly boil, and simply steam for thirty minutes until the rice is tender, white and dry. Turn it into a colander and drain away the last drop of moisture, then throw it on a clean towel or napkin, and, with your hands, spread it out without· breaking the grains. Put three teaspoonfuls of gelatin into half pint of milk and let it soak for fifteen minutes. Put another half pint of milk, with two-thirds of a cup of sugar, into a double boiler; add the grated rind of one lemen and stir until the milk is steaming hot; add the gelatin. Now add the rice to this and turn into a basin. Stand this in another of cracked ice, stir continuously until the mixture begins to thicken, then add carefully and quickly one pint of cream that has been whipped to a stiff froth. Turn this mixture into a border mold and stand it away on the ice.

If it is the strawberry season, have stemmed one quart of fine · berries. Raspberries, peaches or pineapple may be used. The pineapple must be sugared at least a half hour before using. When you are ready to serve the pudding, turn it carefully on a round dish and heap the fruit in the center. If you have pineapple, pour the syrup over the pudding. If you wish to serve this in a solid mold, without fresh fruit, after you have turned it on the serving dish, add a little hot water to a glass of either apple or quince jelly, and stir it over the fire until it becomes slightly liquid, then turn it into a sieve, and hold the sieve over the pudding, and with a spoon stir until the pudding is covered with the jelly. Serve at once.

CARAMEL CUSTARDS

Take eight small custard cups. Put half cup of sugar in a saucepan and stir it over the fire until it melts. When perfectly liquid and a dark straw color, pour in sufficient to cover the bottom of each cup. Beat three eggs without separating; add four tablespoonfuls of sugar and a teaspoonful of vanilla. When well mixed, add one and a half cups of milk. Beat again and turn this mixture into the cups on top of the caramel. Stand the cups in a pan of hot water and bake in the oven until the custard is set in the center. Take from the fire and turn out while hot. The better way is to turn each custard into a saucer on which it is to be served. Stand away until cold, and serve.

CAKE RISSOLES

Cut stale sponge cake into thin slices, then, with a round cutter, into cakes about two inches in diameter. Cover each with almond paste, put two together as you would a sandwich. Dip quickly in egg and crumbs ; fry in hot oil. Serve, with purée of apricots poured over.

COCOANUT MILK

Purchase two fresh cocoanuts; grate them, put the grated cocoanut into a bowl and pour over one quart of boiling water. Allow it to stand until cool. Then, with your hand, press all the liquid out of the cocoanut. Wring the cocoanut carefully, a handful at a time, and put into a bowl. Strain the milk thus produced through a cheese cloth and stand away until the cream comes to the surface. This will take about two hours. Wash the cocoanut with another quart of boiling water; proceed as before, strain and stand aside. Throw the cocoanut away.

CUCUMBER SAUCE

This sauce is exceedingly nice served with either broiled, boiled or creamed fish. Peel and grate four good-sized cucumbers. Put the pulp in a sieve and allow the water to drain carefully away. Then put the pulp in a bowl; add a teaspoonful of grated onion, dash of cayenne, half teaspoonful of salt and, if you have it at hand, a tablespoonful of chopped green pepper. Turn this mixture into the serving dish, add four tablespoonfuls of thick cocoanut cream, tablespoonful of lemon juice and it is ready to use.

CEYLON TOMATO SAUCE

This is a delicious sauce to serve with thin, cold roasted beef or mutton. Select three good-sized solid tomatoes. Remove the skins, cut them into halves, press out the seeds and stand the tomatoes aside until perfectly cold. When ready to use, chop them fine, add half teaspoonful of salt, grain of red pepper and teaspoonful of onion juice or grated onion. Mix and put into the serving dish. Carefully remove the cream from the top of the first bowl of cocoanut milk. Pour four tablespoonfuls of this cream over the tomato; sprinkle over a tablespoonful of lemon juice and it is ready to serve. One table-spoonful of chopped green pepper, and one of green ginger, is an improvement.

CURRIED RICE

Wash one cup of rice through several cold waters, rubbing it well between the hands. Then throw it into a large kettle of boiling water and boil rapidly for thirty minutes. Strain in a colander and stand the colander in the oven for a few minutes until the rice is perfectly dry and white. While the rice is boiling put two tablespoonfuls of butter into a saucepan and add one onion, sliced. Stir constantly until the onion is a golden color, but not brown. Now add a level table-spoonful of flour. Mix carefully with the butter and add half pint of cocoanut milk. Stir until boiling, then add a teaspoonful of turmeric, teaspoonful of curry, moistened in a little cocoanut milk ; bring to boiling point again, and add a half teaspoonful of salt. Dish the rice; strain and curry over, and it is ready to serve.

CEYLON TOMATOES

Scald **and** peel six solid tomatoes. Press out the seeds. Put the tomatoes into a saucepan, add a bay leaf, a slice of onion, clove or garlic, chopped fine. Now cover the tomatoes with the cocoanut milk. Moisten a teaspoonful of turmeric in a little cocoanut milk, add to the tomatoes and cover the saucepan. Cook slowly for fifteen minutes. The tomatoes must remain in perfect halves. Have ready the serving dish, heated, lift the tomatoes carefully, without breaking, and put them on the dish. Now add to the sauce one tablespoonful of butter and one of flour rubbed together.

33

Stir until boiling ; add a teaspoonful of salt, quarter of a teaspoonful of pepper and two teaspoonfuls of lemon juice. Strain this sauce over the tomatoes and serve.

PURÉE OF APRICOTS

Press through a sieve twelve halves of apricots. Put this in a saucepan, adding half cup of the strained liquor from the can. When boiling, add one teaspoonful of arrow-root which has been moistened in a little cold water. Boil a moment, take from fire and add two tablespoonfuls of sherry.

RAGLETS

Put half pint of water and two ounces of butter in a saucepan over the fire. When boiling, add four ounces of flour; beat until a ball of dough is formed. Take from fire, and stand aside to cool. When cool, add one egg, without separating or beating; mix, add another, mix again, and so continue until you have added four eggs. Now beat four or five minutes. Have ready a deep pan of hot fat (oil preferable). Put the mixture into a pastry bag with star tube; press it out into smoking fat, making the ragle.as nearly as possible the shape of small pretzel. Cook on one side, then turn and cook the other. Have ready a dusting material made from a half cup of powdered sugar, one teaspoonful of cinnamon and one of vanilla sugar. Lift the raglets from the fat, drain a moment and then dust well with the mixture. These are very good and must be served the same day on which they are made.

CPSIA information can be obtained
at www.ICGtesting.com
Printed in the USA
LVHW031637281118
598533LV00023B/1175/P